My Name Is...
Leonardo da Vinci

BARRON'S

© Copyright 2006 of English translation by Barron's Educational Series, Inc. for the United States, its territories and possessions, and Canada.

Original title of the book in Spanish: *Me llamo...Leonardo da Vinci*
© 2004 Parramón Ediciones, S.A.,—World Rights
Published by Parramón Ediciones, S.A., Barcelona, Spain

Name of the author of the text: Antonio Tello
Name of the illustrator: Johanna A. Boccardo

Translated from the Spanish by Eric A. Bye, M.A.

Project and Production: Parramón Publishing
Editorial Director: Lluís Borràs
Editorial Assistant: Cristina Vilella
Text: Antonio Tello
Illustrations: Johanna A. Boccardo
Graphic Design and Layout: Zink Communications, Inc.
Production Director: Rafael Marfil
Production: Manel Sánchez

All inquiries should be addressed to:
Barron's Educational Series, Inc.
250 Wireless Boulevard
Hauppauge, New York 11788
www.barronseduc.com

ISBN-13: 978-0-7641-3392-3
ISBN-10: 0-7641-3392-6

Library of Congress Catalog Card No.: 2005929511

Printed in Spain
9 8 7 6 5 4 3 2 1

Hello...

I lived in the second half of the fifteenth century, which we Italians call the *quattrocento*, and part of the following century. This period is known as the Renaissance because it involved the *rebirth* of culture, the arts, and the sciences in Europe. All these human activities sprang back to life with an intensity they hadn't experienced since the time when Roman civilization flourished.

All of us—from philosophers to poets, architects to painters, kings and popes to the common people—felt that we were capable of transforming the world. As a son of this wonderful time period, I too believed in change and progress. That's why I devoted my life to painting and sculpting and to designing fortresses, engines of war, devices for flying, and other small items that simplified people's tasks.

In addition to observing the stars, I studied the human body and devoted considerable time to music (I enjoyed playing the lute), to cooking and preparing banquets, and even to inventing riddles to amuse the ladies of the court. After all, a Renaissance man was supposed to observe and experiment with everything if he wanted to make the world a better place.

Some ideas

that gave rise to the modern world

I lived in a historic time in which ideas changed the world. The main location of these new ideas was in northern Italy, specifically in Florence, my hometown. The idea of a perfect, closed world that had dominated all of the Middle Ages had started to give way a century before. The old, medieval idea no longer served to explain the world, nor an increasingly complex reality; that's what gave rise to what became known as humanism.

Humanism isn't a doctrine, but rather an attitude that people assume in facing reality. What I mean is that people were no longer satisfied to be told "that's the way things are, and that's all there is to it." Those people wanted to know more about themselves, their origins, their place in the universe, and their destiny, so that they could explain the things that were happening to themselves and to others.

On the basis of those questions there arose a belief that human progress could change the world. This was the principle of the social, political, cultural, scientific, and artistic transformations that characterized my time, and which together came to be known as the Renaissance.

Historically speaking, things were changing at a rapid pace. In 1453, when I was barely a year old, the Turks conquered Byzantium, the last stronghold of the Eastern Roman Empire, and France and England ended the Hundred Years' War. Shortly thereafter, the kingdoms of Castile and Aragon in Spain united to form a powerful state, and they prepared to expel the Muslims from the Iberian Peninsula. The European world was changing at a dizzying speed.

Even before that, twelve years before I was born, a German named Gutenberg invented the movable-type printing press. Printing was a true revolution for the diffusion of knowledge. Thanks to that invention, printed books and the ideas they contained could reach

a greater number of people. More people could learn more things. At the same time, merchants were opening new commercial routes and were becoming more powerful in the cities. In the north of Italy, the cities of Venice, Florence, Genoa, and Milan were powerful business centers; they were not governed by kings, but rather by rich merchants and bankers. They formed a social class that was called the bourgeoisie.

Looking at the World Through New Eyes

At the start of the fifteenth century, the cities had been converted into centers of political, economic, and cultural activities. They became places where poets and writers such as Dante Alighieri, Petrarch, and Bocaccio, architects such as Filarete and Leon Battista Alberti, and thinkers such as Coluccio Salutatti were defining the idea that human conduct, reinforced by reason, could direct the destiny of every one of us and of the community.

What the first humanist thinkers instilled in us was that we must aspire to progress and universality, an opening of the minds, by relying on reason:

These two themes would come to define the modern world. As young people born in the middle of the fifteenth century, we hoped for the creation of a more just and harmonious society. The humanists defended individuality, the value of all human beings. Therefore, humanist culture sought to struggle against the tyranny and oppression of bad governments. As the architect Alberti said, "People can do everything, if they want to."

We Renaissance people believed in universal harmony, both in philosophy and politics. We considered the Greek and Roman past as a rebuilding of this harmony. Since that world was now ended, could a new world begin? We were convinced that knowledge could give humankind all the skills needed to transform the world.

Suddenly the world didn't look to us like a vale of tears or an ugly or incomprehensible place, but rather like an organism filled with life. We had to look at the world through new eyes, because everything was alive and full of vitality and virtue. We were convinced that knowledge could provide humankind with all the energies needed to transform the world and adapt to new social situations. Knowledge was power. But it was essential to *saper videre*, that is, to know how to see and observe. Learning to see, to observe, and experiment thus became a skill. This was the secret of all mechanical inventions and artistic creations.

My Sweet Youth

My youth was sweet in many ways, but especially because I had a stepfather who was a pastry chef and made very delicious treats. I was born in Vinci, a small town in Tuscany very close to Florence, Italy, on April 15, 1452. In the Italian language, the "da" after one's first name means "from." Thus, I was from Vinci. My biological father was a rich and well-known Florentine named Ser Piero, and my mother was a beautiful peasant girl named Catherine de Anchiano. A few months after my birth, my father married a Florentine teenager, and my mother married Accatabriga di Piero del Vacca, the pastry chef in Vinci.

I spent my childhood halfway between poverty and wealth. My stepfather, the pastry chef, showed me his trade and passed on to me a taste for sweets and good food, and my father gave me a good education, along with my stepbrothers. However, I didn't have access to Latin, much less to Greek; in time, that lack would weigh heavily on me because I wasn't able to read many of the books by the sages of antiquity. As a result, all my life I spoke and wrote in Tuscan, just as the great Dante Alighieri had done in his *Divine Comedy*.

For amusement I learned to play the lute and sing beautiful ballads. I also began to make up riddles and to draw. My father liked the drawings, and said that with such talent I should study painting and sculpture in the studio of a friend of his in Florence. Like all fathers, mine wanted me to learn to do something useful as soon as possible. So he spoke with his friend, and in 1469 I became a painter's apprentice.

It turned out that the master was the painter and sculptor Andrea del Verrocchio, who was very well known and had many commissions. He really was knowledgeable, and when I was seventeen, I wanted to learn everything. From Verrocchio I learned all the secrets of working and casting metals. He taught me how to create paintings and statues and to study nude and clothed models and interesting plants and animals. The master also taught me the laws of perspective and color technique. Later on, some people said that when I entered his studio, I was a child prodigy who already knew all the secrets of art. But that was just an exaggeration.

The Glutton's Punishment

My stepfather didn't forget me while I was in Verrocchio's studio. He almost always found a way to send me as many cakes and sweets as I wanted every day. It's no wonder that the other apprentices called me "the little fat boy of Vinci," and that master Verrocchio scolded me for gluttony.

When I went to Verrocchio's studio, he designed a helmet in the shape of a dragon. The work was a commission from Giuliano de Medici for display in one of the celebrations that lasted for several days, in which both rich and common folks feasted. The only one who shared my taste for sweets and good food was Sandro Botticelli. Yes, he was the same man who later gained fame with such beautiful paintings as *Springtime* and *The Birth of Venus.*

With Sandro I would go to taverns to eat, drink, play the lute, and sing. At other times we had to work in the kitchens to earn a little extra money.

I don't know why, but our adventures in the taverns of Florence made master Verrocchio very angry since he thought I was a glutton.

Around that time, master Verrocchio was working on a commission from the Church of San Salvi, a *Baptism of Christ*. For punishment of my gluttony, he had me paint an angel holding up some clothing while John the Baptist baptized Jesus. People said that my angel turned out better than the rest of the painting, and that from that time on, Verrocchio acknowledged my superiority and gave up painting. But that's not true. It is true that the other apprentices stopped calling me the "fat boy of Vinci" and that I gained the master's respect. But it's also true that he continued with his studio and that I still respected him. The painting of the *Annunciation* that we finished around 1475 was the product of our collaboration, although many people later attributed it to me alone.

I Want to Be a Free Artist

The most important thing for a Renaissance artist was to feel free. I wanted to be free to see the world, to enjoy life, and to create my own work. However, I still had lots to learn before becoming free, and I felt very impatient because I wanted to know everything.

In 1472 I enrolled in the San Lucas painters' guild. This was an essential step in gaining recognition from others as a painter. But I never got any commissions, and I had to continue as an employee in Verrocchio's studio. The only work that was totally mine at that time was a landscape. Almost no one painted or drew only landscapes at that time. Later, in 1475, I painted *The Madonna of the Carnation*, which was the first work that I consider to be truly mine.

In the meantime, Botticelli and I worked at serving food in the Three Snails Tavern, next to the Ponte Vecchio in Florence. Later on, the owner of the tavern hired us as cooks, but we got fired after a couple of days. In any case, it was a very interesting experience.

Florence was a very lively city, and all the artists had frequent work. Sandro Botticelli started to get major commissions from important people, like the ones from Antonio del Pollaudiolo and Domenico Ghirlandaio, Michelangelo's teacher. However, I had to be content with small jobs. As always happens in art, in order to succeed you need more than talent, you also need good contacts.

I spoke to my father, and thanks to his intervention I got my first important commission: painting a tableau for the chapel of San Bernardo in the Palazzo Vecchio. They gave me a good advance, and I began work. However, when the Three Snails burned down, Botticelli and I dropped everything to open a new tavern. But the business didn't even last two months. Rich and poor alike preferred heaping portions to the nicely decorated dishes we made.

My father helped me once again, and the monks of the Augustine Scopeto Monastery commissioned me to do *The Adoration of the Magi* for the major altar of the church of San Donato. But I left that one unfinished, too, because I decided to move to Milan for a change of scenery.

An Open Window to Reality

The architect Leon Battista Alberti used to say that painting was an open window to reality. Despite my youth, I believed this as well. The painter illustrates the truth of what we see and what we then describe in words about the painting. The laws of perspective convey this reality to the observer.

What are the laws of perspective? Well, from our own point of view, perspective allows us to see and feel an impression of volume, body, and location in space. This makes it possible for us to visualize more dimensions of an object, or depth, rather than simply a flat surface view. On that basis I really began to focus on the painting *The Adoration of the Magi.*

In those years I also realized that I had to devote myself to portraits—not only because the rich families paid very well for them, but also because portraits allowed me to demonstrate that human faces are expressions of the character of every person. I admired the Flemish masters such as Jan van Eyck, Roger van der Weyden, and Hans Memling, who had managed, through the luminosity of their colors, to capture the inner life of their subjects in vibrant portraits.

However, I thought it was possible to go even farther and to show the states of mind of the people in the portraits. I don't know how many notebooks I filled throughout my life with studies of faces and hands. I wanted to achieve perfection and leave a suggestion of the soul in my paintings. I trusted only what I could see with my eyes. If I was in doubt, I experimented. My mission was to explore the world in a way different from that of the Venetian, Genovese, Florentine, Portuguese, and Spanish artists whose paintings did not always express this inner life.

Even though I had already begun with a kneeling *Saint Jerome* whose face was racked with suffering, my first serious attempt to follow this route would be the portrait I did of *Ginebra Benci*.

I painted this portrait using luminous colors, and I included a detailed representation of nature in the manner of the Flemish masters. Detailed though it was, the nature that I painted was symbolic, and it represented the relationship that exists between virtue and beauty.

My Departure for Milan

When I turned thirty, I realized that I needed to give my career as a painter a boost. There were lots of things happening in the world, and in Florence it seemed like I was going nowhere. I spent many days seated in the streets and the taverns of Florence playing the lute and making up enigmas and riddles.

Then the Pazzis, a rich Florentine family, conspired against the Medicis. Juliano de Medici died in their attempt to take control of Florence, but Lorenzo de Medici survived, and he was acclaimed by the people. They called him "Lorenzo the Magnificent."

When they hanged Bernardo di Baudino, the murderer of Juliano, I painted Baudino's portrait and recorded the details of his death. Almost immediately, Rome declared war on Florence, and I offered my services to Lorenzo de Medici as a military engineer. I sent him several designs of fortresses and engines of war, and I included some models made of pasta and marzipan so he would appreciate my ideas more.

But Lorenzo the Magnificent thought they were merely sweets given as a gift, and he had them served to dinner guests. At that point I'd had enough, and I decided on a change of scenery with my friend Atalante Migliorotti, a musician. I chose Milan because Duke Ludovico Sforza had started a competition to sculpt an equestrian statue in honor of his father.

Perhaps by way of excusing himself for eating my marzipan models, Lorenzo de Medici gave me a letter of introduction to Ludovico Sforza. But since I was curious by nature, I opened it, and I read that he was recommending me only as a lute strummer. I tore up that letter and wrote another one.

In my letter I introduced myself as the best builder of bridges, fortifications, catapults, and many other devices that I didn't dare to commit to paper. In times of war, construction engineers have lots of prestige. I also brazenly assured him that I was also a great painter and sculptor. I also added that I was a master in devising riddles and enigmas, and finally, that I could make cakes better than anyone else.

When Ludovico the Moor, as the duke of Milan was nicknamed, read this shameless letter, he wanted to meet me. To the surprise of many, including me, I left the audience hall with the jobs of Counselor of Fortifications and Master of Celebrations and Banquets for the Sforza court.

The Statue I Never Made

When I arrived in Milan, I immediately got in touch with the builders of the cathedrals in that city and in Pavia. I gave them a series of suggestions about their constructions, but they didn't pay any attention to me. At that time the artisans' guilds were very powerful, and they didn't allow anyone who wasn't part of the trade to interfere with their matters.

Amid this scene, I focused on creating the equestrian statue that the duke wanted in honor of his father, Francesco Sforza. Then I thought of the wonderful statue that master Verrocchio had sculpted of General Colleioni for the Venetians. But, as always, I wanted to go beyond that.

I designed a statue almost twenty-five feet high. I had never planned such a huge figure. What's more, I had never tried to create an equestrian statue with a rearing horse, as I now intended to do. It was no easy job, for the tremendous weight created stability problems that forced me to find precisely the right way to hold everything up.

But I have always believed that there is no technical or artistic problem that can't be solved by studying and observing. And that was true. I had also learned that people of accomplishment rarely sat back and let things happen to them.

In 1492 I thought I had everything ready, and I made a clay model nearly the same size as the intended statue. The following year, in my capacity as Master of Celebrations and Banquets, I chose to use it to decorate the wedding party of Bianca Maria Sforza, the duke's niece, when she married Emperor Maximilian. For the occasion I also made enormous palaces and cathedrals of marzipan and gelatin.

As the one in charge of table etiquette, I had invented the napkin so that the people would not wipe their hands and mouth on other people's clothing. I also instructed them in the use of the fork, which the Medicis were already using, although I added a third tine. This fork was very useful for eating the *spago mangiabile*, or edible strands of pasta, which later became known as spaghetti.

But to return to the equestrian statue of Francesco Sforza—sad
to say, it never got made. The bronze intended for it was used to
manufacture cannons.

My Passion for Machines

My passion for mechanical devices came from my conviction that they could make people's lives easier. However, I also realized that at that time, war played a major role in technical invention. This is why I designed fortresses, complex defense systems, siege weapons, auto-loading cannons, repeating crossbows, armored war vehicles, and other wagons with movable cutting blades, which Ludovico put to use against the French.

But engines of war were not my only inventions. I also came up with countless useful devices; if they didn't work, it was only because there weren't enough materials and technical know-how available. For example, I created a two-wheeled vehicle that later would become known as a bicycle, plus an underwater diving suit. I believed that by understanding how each separate machine part worked, I could modify them and combine them in different ways to improve existing machines or to create inventions that no one had ever seen before.

I also told myself that since birds could fly with their wings, and ships could move on rivers and oceans with their sails, why shouldn't people be able to do the same? So I focused on studying the flight of birds and insects, and I drew a device that made it possible to fly by means of rotating helices, and another with jointed wings. While my flying devices could not be put into practical use during my own time (after all, who was ready for my vast ideas?), my plans embodied sound principles of aerodynamics. In addition,

I designed a series of energy-saving devices to make domestic chores easier. I thus made the corkscrew, the peppermill, a spool for winding spaghetti, a dishwasher, an automatic roaster that used hot air to make the spit revolve, and many other things. I suppose you could say that I developed a new attitude about machines in my day, and that was as important to me as anything else I accomplished.

Observing the laws of nature is essential for creating the means that people need to gain mastery over nature. I was convinced that the human hand and intelligence are the instruments that will guarantee our power over the natural world.

The Secrets of Nature

For Renaissance artists, humans and nature were the main topics for artistic creation. Whatever subject we chose, whether religious or secular, our intent was to communicate a reality in which people's sentiments were revealed in harmony with their moral qualities. That's why it was important for us to convey an understanding of the inner shapes of humans.

To transmit all the reality of the world in which we live, we artists had to know how to see it and interpret it. Since it was essential that we thoroughly know the laws of nature, I attempted to discover all of its secrets. As I've already mentioned, I studied the flight of birds and insects with a view toward making flying machines. Once you have tasted flight, you will walk the earth with your eyes turned skyward, for there you were and there you will long to return.

I also tried to learn the laws that moved the waves and impelled ocean currents, and the laws that governed the growth of trees and plants. On every excursion to the country, I would stop to observe the shapes that surrounded me in nature.

I could spend hours and hours trying to figure out why atmospheric changes altered the color of distant objects, and where the secret of the harmony of sounds was hidden.

I didn't intend to turn into a scientist by doing this. My goal was to know more about the reality of the world so I could apply it to my art. All art needs a scientific basis so that the reality it represents is as close as possible to the reality we experience. I mean that humankind, the world, and the universe make up a single harmonious entity, and it is the artist's mission to discover the laws that govern that harmony. I have been impressed with the urgency of doing. Knowing is not enough; we must apply our knowledge. Being willing is not enough; we must do.

I must admit that it was also my goal that the art of painting should be considered a noble activity. Ever since ancient times, all work done with the hands had been considered low-class. Artists were considered mere servants, but we artists were not servants, and art was not a low-class activity. Just as the poet needs a pen for writing poems, a painter needs a brush for painting pictures.

As a Renaissance man, I stood up for my individual liberty. I didn't allow anyone else to control my tastes and my ideas, and the people who commissioned me to create a work had no right to decide when I must complete it. As the artist, I was the one to decide when the work was done.

If I wrote backwards, it was because I was left-handed. My writing could be read only with the aid of a mirror, but it was not because I wanted to hide anything. I did it to show that the

artists are the ones who make the rules for viewing and interpreting their works. I invented this special writing myself, and I wrote in the normal direction only when I was writing something intended for other people. People in the future have argued about why I used this "mirror writing." Some said I was trying to make it harder for people to read my notes and steal my ideas. Others believed I was using a code to hide some scientific ideas from the Catholic Church, whose teachings I sometimes disagreed with. What do you think? If you're left-handed, is your writing "mirror writing?"

My Studies of the Human Body

As I have already noted, the organic shapes of nature and of human beings were the main motifs for artistic creation among Renaissance artists. We felt obliged to express our faith in humankind and in nature in an intimate and profound way. In other words, we had to be capable of transmitting the rhythm of the universe as a creation of God.

By turning our gaze to the classical art of ancient Greece and Rome, we hoped to restore that harmony between humankind, their works, and the world. We thus imagined perfect cities, we applied the laws of perspective, and we also studied the human body and animals.

It makes sense that we had to know the perfection of the human body in order for the people that we painted or sculpted to express all their greatness. To that end, our duty was to observe, study, and experiment. First, because imagination is not as reliable as the eye. Second, because experience itself is the mother of truth. Experience is like a ship of sailors who venture into the ocean, discovering new routes, lands, and people they never imagined existed.

The territories of the human body that I discovered are represented by its muscles, its veins, its vital organs, its brain, and its bones. And I drew the human body in all naturalness. The reason is that if you want to know all of human anatomy, you have to look at it from several different angles.

My anatomical drawings reflect everything that I saw—the branching of the veins as well as the spiritual qualities—and the muscles, tendons, and veins in the arm and the leg, the skeleton and the skull, the intestines and the heart. I am sure that I learned much more than any doctor of my time. Unfortunately, the doctors continued to cling to the old science and manuals for a long time. Also, since I realized that the human body had a lot in common with animals, I studied them both and compared them. I even believed that the horse skeleton had a structure similar to the human skeleton.

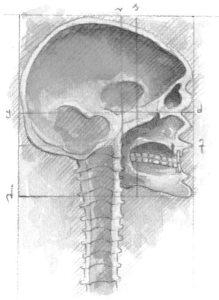

The Perfect Human Body

Renaissance artists created a type of art that used humans as the central focus. Space and objects were only backgrounds for the human figure. We moved on from the classical forms, and we used the laws of perspective and the measurement of proportion in drawing the human body.

One day it occurred to me to look at objects through glass and against the light. It was astonishing. I understood the relationship that exists between perspective and calculating the measurements of the human body in its true proportions. I already knew of its importance, but I wasn't certain until I did that simple experiment.

Around 1489, while I was working on the equestrian statue of Francesco Sforza, I set out to study anatomy, physiology, and the proportions of the human body in depth. I drew and wrote down everything I observed in a notebook that I entitled *On the Human Body*. How did I accomplish this?

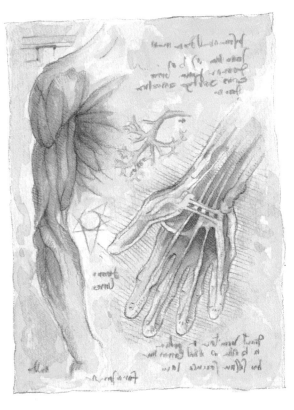

To begin with, I spent several months taking the measurements of two young men until I had a set of proportions for the human body. Once I had the results, I compared them to the Vitruvian man. And who was the Vitruvian man?

Vitruvius was an architect from the time of the Roman Empire who had drawn the perfect human body. According to him, a man with arms and legs extended could be situated inside the perfect geometric figures of the circle and the square.

Some of my contemporaries took measurements in accordance with medieval religious geometry. But that resulted in hands that were too large and feet that were excessively long. I ignored not only that geometry, but also the geometrical relationships between square and circle. What I did was start with my own measurements.

In the end I corrected the errors of Vitruvius and established the proportions for the perfect man. I agreed with Vitruvius that the center of the man in the circle is located at the navel; however, that doesn't apply to the man in the square, in whom the center is located just above the groin. Many artists considered the knowledge of the human body to be very useful but never had the precise measurements. I accomplished this for them.

The Virgin of the Rocks

The same year in which I arrived in Milan and entered into the service of Duke Ludovico the Moor, the Brotherhood of the Immaculate Conception commissioned me to create an altarpiece for the altar of the Chapel of the Virgin in the Church of San Francisco Grande. The Predis brothers also helped to paint other parts of the scene. My job was to paint the Virgin for the door of the niche where a wooden sculpture of the Virgin and the Child were kept; they were brought out every December 8, the celebration day of the Immaculate Conception.

Although the job paid well, I wasn't attracted to it at the time because I was very busy with the equestrian statue of the duke's father and with my anatomical studies. But since I didn't want

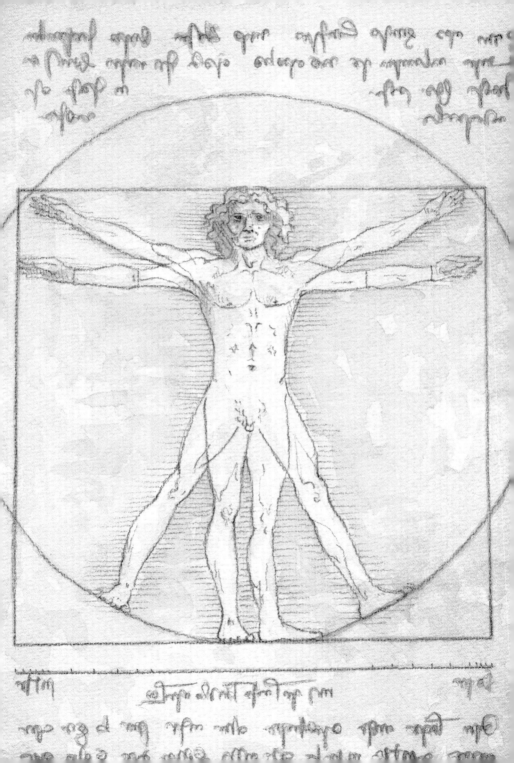

to lose the commission, I offered the Franciscans a painting of the Virgin that I had already completed. However, the measurements weren't right and needed to be corrected. The Franciscans were very generous in allowing me to paint the same picture; that's why there are two versions of *The Virgin of the Rocks*.

I say that I appreciated the generosity of the Brotherhood, because it was not common to paint a very young Mary with Saint John the Baptist, the Christ child, and an angel. There is no mention in the Bible of a meeting between John the Baptist and the child Jesus, but it is mentioned in texts that are not accepted by the Church. According to those apocryphal texts, the meeting took place when Herod ordered the killing of children and forced the Holy Family to flee to Egypt.

The scene refers to this meeting in very dramatic circumstances. So I attempted to highlight the protective gesture by the Virgin and the relationship among all the characters through gestures and glances. If you recall, in the first version (the one with the darker background, in which the children have no

halos, and John the Baptist doesn't have the staff with the cross), the angel looks toward us and incorporates us into the scene.

In the two versions, the people appear to be at the edge of a ravine. I meant this to suggest that even though they are close, they are beyond our reach. That is also suggested by the rocky landscape of the grotto, the mountains covered with fog, and the water. In the second version, I modified this part of the painting and painted a patch of blue sky so that its light on the characters, the rocks, and the vegetation would create a greater sensation of warmth.

Finally, a Studio Painter

The prestige I gained from *The Virgin of the Rocks* was not enough to convince the duke to make me his studio painter. Even though I was in service to him, Ludovico Sforza didn't commission me to do any paintings. But since I knew that all things come to pass, I prepared myself by doing hundreds of studies of the heads and faces of men, women, and young and old people.

In 1490, Ludovico commissioned me to paint a portrait of Cecilia Gallerani, who was his lover. In the portrait I painted of her, which is known as the *Lady with the Ermine*, I continued to follow the guidelines of the Flemish masters.

I painted Cecilia's body at an angle to the surface of the painting, and this created a unique dynamism—accentuated by the gesture of the ermine, which mimics that of the girl, whose hand, in turn, reflects the movement of the animal.

Also, since I'm a man devoted to coming up with riddles and playing with symbols, there are several in this painting. For example, the ermine has several meanings. One of them is that the word *ermine* in Greek sounds very similar to Gallerani, the girl's family name. Another is that the ermine is a symbol of virtue. But most important, it was one of the symbols of the Sforza family. So I was very happy to place the animal identified with Ludovico in Cecilia's arms as she caresses it gently.

The Last Supper

The marriage of the duke to Beatrice d'Este was good for me. Beatrice liked my riddles and found them very amusing. Also she very much liked a portrait I painted of her. I have always thought that it was through the intervention of Ludovico's wife that he convinced the brothers of the Monastery of Santa Maria delle Grazie to commission me, in 1495, to paint a fresco in their dining room of *The Last Supper*.

From the very beginning, I felt that this would be one of my best works. Guided by that feeling, I went to the monastery with my apprentices and began to contemplate and study the composition of the mural, since the painting had to be done on the wall. For nearly two years I kept thinking about it, until the monks complained to Ludovico.

They said that my assistants and I were drinking up all their wine and eating all their food. That was partly true, but I wanted to be sure of the food and the type of wine to put on

the table. I wanted to know the texture, the taste, and the color of the foods and the wine of that dinner before painting. I wanted to know exactly how the apostles would be arranged around Jesus, and precisely what their facial expressions would be when he told them, "In truth, I tell you that one of you will betray me." What a moment!

And it was worth reflecting and experimenting for two years. I achieved a wonderful effect. The depiction, as if on a large stage, was unlike any of the "Last Suppers" that had been painted up to that time. This involved not only realism, but it also made visible the effect that Christ's words produced on the apostles. As in the biblical text, the disciples of Jesus question one another, and this questioning and answering is what brings the observer into the heart of the scene.

Look at the resigned face of Christ and his open hands. Look at the faces of the apostles, and note that the only one who remains silent, tense, and somewhat pushed aside by Peter is Judas.

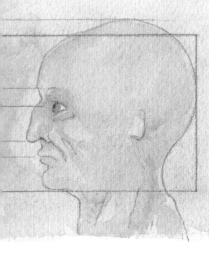

Judas appears to be waiting for Christ to say his name as he presses the purse containing the coins of betrayal.

The monks were very surprised by the mural of *The Last Supper*, and the duke himself came with his court to see it.

The Fall of Ludovico the Moor

I was feeling very happy with my new situation. The duke commissioned me to decorate the Sala delle Asse, but as the saying goes, happiness doesn't last in the house of a poor man. My luck changed. In 1499, the duke's political problems grew, and the fragile balance of peace between France and Italy changed. French troops defeated Ludovico the Moor and entered Milan, and I was without a patron.

Louis XII really liked *The Last Supper* and *The Virgin of the Rocks,* and the French king gave me a commission. He wanted me to paint a picture including Saint Ann, the Virgin, Saint John the Baptist, and Jesus to give as a gift to his wife, Anne of Brittany. But I only did a sketch, which is known as the *Burlington House Cartoon.*

I left for Mantua and sought shelter in the court of Isabella d'Este. Isabella, who composed beautiful songs, wanted me to paint a portrait of her. In February of 1500 I made a charcoal sketch, drawing her in profile in the traditional style of Mantua, and tried to highlight her social status and serene spirit.

Soon I left for Venice, where I did some minor works, and then to Florence. But I wasn't happy in Florence, either, or satisfied with what I was doing. At that time I was drawn to geometry and mathematics. Florimond Robertet, the secretary of the French king, commissioned me to do a painting, and I painted the *Madonna of the Spindle* for him. But as soon as I finished it, I left Florence and entered into the service of Cesar Borgia, duke of Romagna, as a military engineer. It was a novel experience. He was the illegitimate son of Pope Alexander VI, and for him I designed fortresses and made maps as if they were landscapes from a bird's-eye view; these turned out to be very useful. But I didn't stay with Borgia very long, and I returned to Florence at the start of 1503.

The Mona Lisa, the Lady with the Smile

The *Mona Lisa*, or *La Gioconda*, is the most famous of my paintings. Much has been said about the girl who seems to be looking at us and smiling enigmatically—as if she were playing with us or knew something that we don't. Some people said that she was a peasant girl; others said this was a boy, or that it was even a modified self-portrait.

The woman in this painting is Lisa del Giocondo, the wife of Francesco del Giocondo, a rich Florentine merchant. This is Madona Lisa, or if you prefer, Mona Lisa Gioconda.

Well, I started to paint *La Gioconda* in the spring of 1503, one year after the Genovese navigator Christopher Columbus began his fourth voyage to that unknown continent, America, which he had discovered in 1492.

The truth is that I never delivered the picture to the person who commissioned it, and I kept making corrections for years. I used many resources in the portrait of this woman so that the painting would communicate different emotions to the observers, without ever sacrificing the true nature of the person. I wanted a painting that would be lively and intense, with a certain mystery.

Ever since I had painted *The Adoration of the Magi*, I was certain that in order to achieve that effect of life and mystery it was necessary to leave some things up to the observer's imagination. So I tried to not paint the outlines perfectly, and to paint the shapes of the face and the body with soft colors, so they almost got lost in the shadows. I used this technique, which later came to be called *sfumato*, specifically to highlight the expression of the eyes and the corner of the mouth. So, since the outlines of the eyes and the lips are done in *sfumato*, the observer finds the *Mona Lisa*'s expression to be mysterious. But I also did something else in this painting—something very daring for my time. I altered the horizon line in the background and hid the break of the line behind the woman's head. So, since the horizon on the right is higher than the one on the left, if the observer's attention is focused on the left side, the lady appears taller. On the other hand, if the gaze is directed to the right side, Mona Lisa appears shorter. Even her face seems to be altered with the change in position.

Of course there's much more, but those things come up thanks to the imagination and the sensitivity of the people who look at the painting. Raphael would come to my studio, and he was fascinated by this painting. He was a very sensitive young man and a great artist. But the one I really admired was Michelangelo Buonarroti.

My Meeting with the Great Michelangelo

While I was painting *La Gioconda* I was on a jury that was to evaluate the sculpture of a young artist. This was a great experience, for I was able to admire a wonderful work of art.

This was perhaps one of the most beautiful works of art of all time. I'm referring to Michelangelo's *David*. This young man wasn't content to learn the laws of human anatomy by reading them in books. Michelangelo, like me, studied bodies until he became familiar with the tiniest details of their muscles. His *David* struck me as so wonderful that I used it as a model for many drawings.

The most interesting thing is that fate put us onto the same route. Almost immediately, in the fall of 1503, the Florentine government commissioned us to decorate the Great Council Hall of the Palazzo Vecchio. Michelangelo was to paint the *Battle of Cascina*, and I the *Battle of Anghiari*. It was a real duel between two artists.

Michelangelo put into practice all his talents and his ideas concerning beauty and the sculptural rendition of the male nude, which he had already explored with his *David*. And in truth he produced a very beautiful composition that symbolically expressed the drama of the historic battle of the Florentines.

As for me, I took inspiration from an ancient gem called *The Fall of Phaeton*, which belonged to the Medicis. Based on that composition, I painted the violent battle between the Milanese troops and those of the alliance between Florence and the pope. In this mural I wasn't concerned with victors or losers, but rather the very brutality of war.

In fact, war was what destroyed the murals in the palace before the century was over. The only things left were the copies of our sketches. It's true that I left mine unfinished, because I didn't feel that they paid me enough.

But the experience served to confirm one thing for me. A person, no matter how knowledgeable, always has to be ready to learn from others. In my case, the talent of Michelangelo, who was much younger than I was, taught me some new ways of expression.

In the Court of the King of France

With the help of the French governor of Milan, Charles d'Amboise, I left Florence in May of 1506. In addition to painting some works for my new patron, including *Leda and the Swan*, whose owners later lost it, I focused on decorating for the court celebrations. I also worked as an architect to install an irrigation system—a job that I also performed for the pope during my stay in Rome.

Soon I returned to my studies of anatomy, focused on the system of locomotion, the system that provides us with the ability to move.

When my patron died in 1511, I went into the service of the Florentine Giuliano de Medici, who took me to Rome with him. While I did not receive any significant commissions there, I did try several experiments with paints using the *sfumato* technique.

When Giuliano de Medici died in 1516, I accepted an invitation from King François I. I left Rome, and with my apprentices Francesco Menzi and Giacomo Salai, and my faithful cook, Battista de Villanis, I went to the court of the king of France. We crossed the Alps on the backs of mules and took up residence in the palace of Cloux, which would later be called Close-Luce.

The palace that the king gave me was next to his, in Amboise. There, in the beautiful Loire Valley, I spent the last years of my life. I became friends with the king, a man who was sensitive to art and beauty. He generously appreciated my drawings of animals and mythical creatures, and he was at my side in my last moments. Finally, my days drew to a close on May 2, 1519, at the age of sixty-seven. I had already given all that I could offer, and everything that a man could imagine in that era—the Renaissance, which provided the basis for the modern world. As a well-spent day brings happy sleep, so a life well spent brings a peaceful death.

Years	Leonardo's Life	History
1452–1470	1452 Born in Vinci, April 15. 1460 Studies in Florence. 1469 Begins apprenticeship in the studio of Andrea Verrocchio.	Constantinople falls into the hands of the Turks. Fall of the Eastern Roman Empire. The Italian states sign the peace of Lodi End of the Hundred Years' War.
1471–1480	1472 Paints the angel in the *Baptism of Christ* by Verrocchio. 1475 Paints *The Annunciation* and the *Madonna of the Carnation.* 1478 Opens a tavern with Sandro Botticelli. 1480 Portrait of *Ginebra Benci.*	Conflicts in Florence between the Medicis and the Pazzis, encouraged by Pope Sixtus IV. Unification of the kingdoms of Castile and Aragon. Ivan III defeats the Golden Horde. In America the Incas conquer the kingdom of Chimu.
1481–1490	1481 *The Adoration of the Magi.* 1482 Goes to Milan. 1483 Enters the service of Ludovico Sforza. Paints *The Virgin of the Rocks.* 1485 Designs for engines of war. 1490 Paints *Madona Litta* and *The Lady with the Ermine.* Draws *The Perfect Man.*	Henry VII begins the Tudor dynasty in England. Charles VIII of France conquers Naples. Louis XII of France supports Cesar Borgia.
1491–1500	1491 Continues his anatomy studies. 1492 Clay model for the equestrian statue of Lorenzo Sforza. 1498 Finishes *The Last Supper.*	The Catholic kings conquer Granada and end the Muslim domination of Spain. Milan falls to the French.
1501–1510	1502 Begins *Saint Ann, the Virgin, and the Child.* Enters the service of Cesar Borgia. 1503 Paints the *Mona Lisa* using the *sfumato* technique. Begins the mural of *The Battle of Anghiari* in Florence. 1504 Anatomical studies based on Michelangelo's *David.* 1508 Paints a new version of *The Virgin of the Rocks.*	François I accedes to the French throne. Pontificate of Pope Leon X.
1511–1520	1513 Goes to Rome in the service of Giuliano de Medici. Paints *Saint John the Baptist.* 1516 Goes to France at the invitation of François I. 1519 Dies in Cloux, May 2.	Pope Julius II unites the Holy League against the French in Italy. Charles I of Spain becomes Emperor Charles V of the Germanic Holy Roman Empire.

Science

Cosme de Medici supports the founding of the Platonic Academy, focusing on Humanism. Printing is introduced to Italy.

Nicholas Copernicus is born.
The first firearms are made in Turin.
Georg von Peuerback edits *New Planetary Theory* and initiates calendar reform.

Bartholomeu Dias rounds the Cape of Good Hope.
Vasco da Gama reaches India.
The department of Julian philosophy is created in Mallorca.

Christopher Columbus discovers America. Juan de la Cosa draws the first map of America. Martin Waldseemüller publishes the first map of the world and calls the New World America in honor of Amerigo Vespucci.

Erasmus publishes *In Praise of Folly*.
Machiavelli publishes *The Prince*.
Miguel Servet discovers the circulatory system.

Arts

Filarete publishes *Treatise on Architecture*.
Piero della Francesca paints the frescos of Saint Francis of Arezzo.

Jorge Manrique writes *Verses on the Death of His Father*.
Sandro Botticelli paints *Spring*.
Verrocchio creates the equestrian statue of Colleoni.

Botticelli paints *The Birth of Venus*.
Matteo M. Boiardo writes the poem "Orlando in Love."

Michelangelo sculpts the *Pietà*.
La Celestina by Fernando de Rojas is published.

Michelangelo sculpts *David*. He begins decorating the Sistine Chapel.
Raphael paints the *Madonna del Granduca*.

Tintoretto is born.
Titian paints the *Assumption* and *Bacchanal*.
The Commedia dell'Arte appears in Italy.

My Name Is...

is a collection of biographies of people with universal appeal, written for young readers. In each book, a figure from history, science, art, culture, literature, or philosophy writes in an appealing way about his or her life and work, and about the world in which he or she lived. Abundant illustrations, inspired by the historical time period, help us become immersed in the time and the environment.

Leonardo da Vinci

A native of Vinci, a small town in Tuscany in the center of Italy, Leonardo was a painter, sculptor, engineer, architect, inventor, and writer—in other words, a prototype of the Renaissance man. He probably excelled most in painting and sculpture, with ample uses of *chiaroscuro, sfumato*, perspective, expressiveness, and scientific precision. One of his outstanding paintings is the *Mona Lisa* (now in the Louvre, Paris). A relatively small portrait, it is famous for the enigmatic smile that Leonardo created in his depiction of the wife of Francesco del Giocondo; the painting is also referred to as *La Gioconda*.